student
WORKBOOK

GCSE Schools History Project
Enquiry in Depth: Germany, 1919–45
John Collingwood

Philip Allan Updates, an imprint of Hodder Education, an Hachette UK company, Market Place, Deddington, Oxfordshire OX15 0SE

Orders
Bookpoint Ltd, 130 Milton Park, Abingdon, Oxfordshire, OX14 4SB
tel: 01235 827827, fax: 01235 400401
e-mail: education@bookpoint.co.uk
Lines are open 9.00 a.m.–5.00 p.m., Monday to Saturday, with a 24-hour message answering service. You can also order through the Philip Allan Updates website: www.philipallan.co.uk

© Philip Allan Publishers 2006

ISBN 978-1-84489-541-0

Printed in Spain

Hachette UK's policy is to use papers that are natural, renewable and recyclable products and made from wood grown in sustainable forests. The logging and manufacturing processes are expected to conform to the environmental regulations of the country of origin.

Introduction 2

Topic 1 Germany under the Weimar Republic, 1919–29 3

Topic 2 Hitler's rise to power, 1919–33 15

Topic 3 Control and opposition, 1933–45 23

Topic 4 The economy under the Nazis, 1933–45 31

Topic 5 Women and the Church, 1933–45 40

Topic 6 Education and youth movements, 1933–45 50

Topic 7 Propaganda and culture, 1933–45 57

Topic 8 The persecution of Jews and other minority groups, 1933–45 ... 65

Topic 9 Overview 74

Introduction

This workbook is designed to help you prepare for the GCSE examination module Enquiry in Depth: Germany, 1919–45. The content is divided into nine topics. The first two cover the years of the Weimar Republic and Hitler's rise to power. The next six topics cover important aspects of life in Germany under the Nazis. The final topic provides an overview of the whole course.

Within each topic you will find:

- **a summary of essential knowledge**, focusing on changes during the period of study and the main factors that have influenced those changes. These summaries are not intended to cover all the details of a particular theme and should be used with your class notes and textbook.
- **questions and exercises**, which are designed to help you learn and/or revise each topic and also practise the skills that are essential for the examination:
  - the analysis and evaluation of sources
  - the writing of extended answers, using your own knowledge of each topic

Spaces are provided for your answers, which give you some idea of how long each answer should be. The questions are structured so that they increase in difficulty within each topic.

Source questions

When answering source questions there are two important points to remember.

First, don't just **describe** what a written source says, or a picture shows. Try to draw an **inference** or make a **deduction** about the overall meaning or significance of the source. For example, you could be given a picture source such as the one in Topic 2, Question 12, and asked: 'What does Source C tell us about Hitler's rise to power in Germany?'

Many candidates make the mistake of just describing in detail what they can see in the picture. Better candidates start by making an inference and then referring to details in the source to support what they have said, such as 'Source C tells us that Hitler needed the help of other people to get into power. You can tell this because the source shows...'.

Second, if the question tells you to 'use the **source** and your own **knowledge** in your answer' — then make sure you do use both. Try to get into the habit of using the source first and referring to it by its name, i.e. 'Source A' or 'Source B' and so on.

Extended writing

The last question in each topic is designed as an 'extended writing' or essay exercise. You should write your answers to these questions on separate paper. You should end these answers with a separate conclusion. However, do not just summarise what you have already said; you should state an opinion in answer to the question set and support it with a strong point based on your knowledge of the topic.

In the final weeks of the First World War, Germany was in a state of chaos. There were strikes and revolts by workers and soldiers in many towns. Morale was falling rapidly across the country due to food shortages, a flu epidemic and a growing realisation that the war was being lost.

Fearing that he might be overthrown in a violent revolution, the Kaiser abdicated on 9 November 1918 and fled to Holland. A new government was set up under **Friedrich Ebert**, leader of the Social Democratic Party. Following elections on 19 January 1919, a new assembly met at the town of Weimar. Ebert was appointed president of the new **Weimar Republic** and a new **constitution** (which set out how the country was to be governed) was drawn up.

Table 1 Strengths and weaknesses of the Weimar constitution

Strengths	Weaknesses
The head of state, the president, was to be elected every 7 years by the people.	In times of crisis **Article 48** allowed the president to take on extra powers and 'rule by decree', i.e. he could ignore the Reichstag and pass laws himself.
All Germans over the age of 20 were given the vote.	The voting system of **proportional representation (PR)** meant many minor parties won seats in the Reichstag. They tended to represent the concerns of small groups rather than the national interest.
Basic rights like freedom of speech and religion were protected.	The presence of many small parties meant it was hard for one party to have a majority – **coalitions** were inevitable.

This created what has been described as the most democratic system of government Germany had ever had. However, the constitution had weaknesses as well as strengths (see Table 1) and these weaknesses aided the rise of the Nazis from 1930 to 1932.

The Armistice and the Treaty of Versailles

The new republic got off to a bad start because it was associated with defeat in the First World War and the hated Treaty of Versailles.

One of the first acts of Ebert's government, in November 1918, was to sign the **armistice** which brought an end to the fighting in the First World War. Germany was clearly beaten and Ebert had no choice but to do this, but his opponents later created the myth that victory had still been possible and the Weimar politicians were the '**November criminals**' who had '**stabbed the German army in the back**'.

Another blow came in June 1919, when the Weimar government had to agree to the **Treaty of Versailles** (see page 4). Most Germans were bitterly were angry about the treaty.

Once again, Ebert's government had no real choice but to agree to the treaty, as Germany was in no position to restart the fighting. However, signing this 'diktat' (dictated peace) was a major reason for the lack of loyalty towards the Weimar Republic on the part of many Germans until 1933.

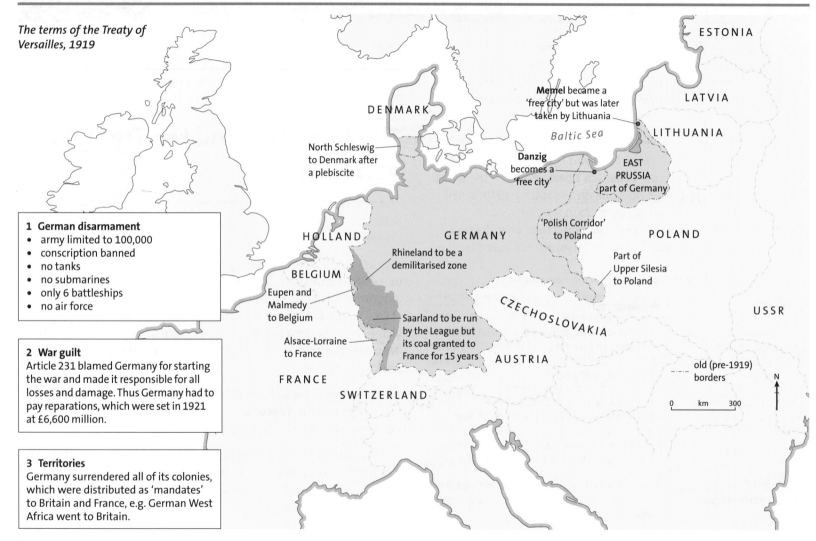

The terms of the Treaty of Versailles, 1919

Memel became a 'free city' but was later taken by Lithuania

North Schleswig to Denmark after a plebiscite

Danzig becomes a 'free city'

EAST PRUSSIA part of Germany

'Polish Corridor' to Poland

Part of Upper Silesia to Poland

Rhineland to be a demilitarised zone

Eupen and Malmedy to Belgium

Alsace-Lorraine to France

Saarland to be run by the League but its coal granted to France for 15 years

ESTONIA · LATVIA · LITHUANIA · DENMARK · *Baltic Sea* · POLAND · USSR · HOLLAND · GERMANY · BELGIUM · CZECHOSLOVAKIA · FRANCE · AUSTRIA · SWITZERLAND

old (pre-1919) borders

0 km 300

N

1 German disarmament
- army limited to 100,000
- conscription banned
- no tanks
- no submarines
- only 6 battleships
- no air force

2 War guilt
Article 231 blamed Germany for starting the war and made it responsible for all losses and damage. Thus Germany had to pay reparations, which were set in 1921 at £6,600 million.

3 Territories
Germany surrendered all of its colonies, which were distributed as 'mandates' to Britain and France, e.g. German West Africa went to Britain.

Political problems

1 The Spartacist Rising, January 1919

Ebert's new government also had to deal with violent opposition in its early days — from both the left and the right of German politics. **Left-wing** groups like the **Spartacists** (who later renamed themselves the Communist Party) thought the changes since November 1918 had not gone far enough. They wanted a full-scale revolution like the one in Russia in 1917 and wanted Germany to be run by workers' councils or soviets.

The Spartacists tried to seize power themselves in January 1919 before the new assembly met at Weimar but, after several days of fighting, their attempt failed. Ebert crushed them using a combination of the regular army and around 4,000 *Freikorps* — ex-soldiers who were strongly anti-Communist. The Spartacist leaders, **Rosa Luxemburg** and **Karl Liebknecht**, were both murdered. Further Communist revolts in 1919 and 1920 were also put down by the *Freikorps*, but the Communist Party remained an important political force in Germany until 1933.

2 The Kapp Putsch, March 1920

Right-wing groups in Germany, such as rich landowners and army generals, disliked the Weimar Republic because it represented too much change from the past. They had little time for democratic institutions and wanted a return to the 'old' Germany with its powerful army and strong leadership under the Kaiser. They saw the *Freikorps* as a useful defence against the growing threat of communism. However, with more and more ex-soldiers joining *Freikorps* units the government grew concerned and began to take steps to disband them.

This resulted in a **putsch** (attempt to overthrow the government) led by **Dr Wolfgang Kapp** in March 1920. He marched into Berlin with 5,000 *Freikorps* soldiers and tried to take control of the city. The army refused to take action against 'fellow soldiers' and the government was forced to flee. However, the workers of Berlin organised a general strike and the city ground to a halt, forcing Kapp to give up. This shows that many people were prepared to back the Weimar government and it survived this crisis, although politically motivated murders continued throughout 1921 and 1922.

3 The Munich Putsch, November 1923

This right-wing attempt by **Adolf Hitler** and his National Socialists to seize power in November 1923 also failed (see Topic 2).

Economic problems

As part of the Treaty of Versailles, Germany was obliged to make **reparations payments** to France and Belgium. In 1921 these were fixed at £6,600 million, to be paid in annual instalments, despite German protests that the figure was far too high.

Although the first instalment was paid, in 1922 the German government said it could not afford to make a further payment. Germany's difficulties were genuine because of debts left over from the First World War and the cost of introducing much-needed welfare reforms. However, in January 1923 French and Belgian troops decided to occupy the Ruhr, Germany's industrial heartland, and take coal and iron ore in place of reparations payments. The

German government retaliated by ordering workers in the **Ruhr** to follow a campaign of **passive resistance**, by refusing to cooperate with the occupying forces. The French reacted by expelling 150,000 people from the region and 132 workers were shot during the following months. Industrial production fell rapidly, leaving the government very short of money.

In an attempt to solve this problem, the government began printing more and more money. Inflation (where money loses its value and buys less) had been growing slowly since 1919. However, the events of 1923 led to **hyperinflation**. Paper money became worthless and many ordinary Germans lost their life savings, although some industrialists were able to pay off huge debts.

Recovery under Stresemann

Germany recovered from the crisis of 1923 and enjoyed a period of prosperity until 1929. This was mainly thanks to the work of **Gustav Stresemann** — chancellor from August and foreign minister from November 1923.

- The campaign of passive resistance to the French in the Ruhr was called off, though many saw this as an act of cowardice. As a result, the French withdrew and normal production in Germany resumed.
- A new currency, the **Rentenmark**, was introduced.
- Loans from the USA were negotiated through the **Dawes Plan** (1924), which also linked reparations payments to Germany's ability to pay.
- The **Young Plan** (1929) reduced Germany's reparations greatly.
- Germany's relations with other countries improved when it signed the **Locarno Treaties** (1925), in which it promised to accept its western border with France and Belgium and use only peaceful means to seek changes to its eastern border. In 1926 Germany joined the League of Nations.

All these changes led to a 'boom' period in Germany from 1924 to 1929, characterised by low unemployment, a stable currency and greater political stability. Artists, film-makers and writers enjoyed great freedom during this period and were able to experiment with new ideas and previously forbidden themes such as antiwar sentiments. Berlin became noted for its jazz bands and nightlife, although crime and prostitution also flourished.

Some problems remained, however:
- There were still regular changes of government and many people became cynical about the deals that political parties made to create coalitions.
- Around 30% of voters continued to support extremist parties such as the Communists and Nazis.
- Ebert died in 1925 and the highly-respected First World War hero **Hindenburg** was elected president — he was not a great supporter of democracy.
- Berlin's nightclubs were seen as evidence of a decline in moral values. They attracted criticism not only from the Church but from many ordinary Germans.
- Economic prosperity was heavily dependent on US loans.
- From 1927, many farmers got into debt because of falling food prices.

This period of prosperity came to an abrupt end in 1929 when the **Wall Street Crash** set off a chain of events that led to 6 million unemployed people by 1933, the rise to power of Adolf Hitler in January 1933, and the end of democracy in Germany soon after.

Questions

Use the information provided, your class notes and your textbook to answer the following questions.

1 Complete the timeline opposite by matching the following jumbled events with the correct dates.

- The Kapp Putsch took place
- The Locarno Treaties were signed
- The Armistice was signed; the First World War ended
- The occupation of the Ruhr began
- Germany joined the League of Nations
- The Wall Street Crash took place
- Stresemann became chancellor
- The Dawes Plan was agreed
- The Treaty of Versailles was signed
- The Spartacist Rising took place

2 What sort of problems was Germany having towards the end of the First World War?

3 Name the new government formed in January 1919 and its first president.

4 Describe **two** strengths and **two** weaknesses of the new constitution.

1

Date	Event
1918 (November)	
1919 (January)	
1919 (June)	
1920	
1923 (January)	
1923 (August)	
1924	
1925	
1926	
1929	

2

....

3

....

4

....

....

....

....

....

5 Why was the new Weimar Republic unpopular with so many Germans?

5

....

....

....

....

6 Describe **three** parts of the Treaty of Versailles that were particularly disliked by most Germans.

6

....

....

....

7 Complete the table summarising opposition to the Weimar Republic 1919–23 by writing your own notes in the blank spaces.

Who opposed Weimar?	Why did they oppose it?	How did they oppose it?	What happened to them?
The Spartacists, 1919			
Dr Kapp and the *Freikorps*, 1920			
The Nazis, 1923 (see Topic 2 for details)			

Questions

8 Arrange the events listed below in their correct chronological order to create a flow chart showing the causes of the inflation crisis of 1923.

- The government ordered workers in the Ruhr to follow a campaign of passive resistance; production fell rapidly.
- As part of the Treaty of Versailles, Germany had to start reparations payments in 1921.
- Hyperinflation was the result; paper money was worthless.
- In January 1923, French and Belgian troops occupied the Ruhr.
- To try to solve Germany's problems, the government printed more and more paper money.
- In 1922, the German government said it could not afford to make reparations payments.

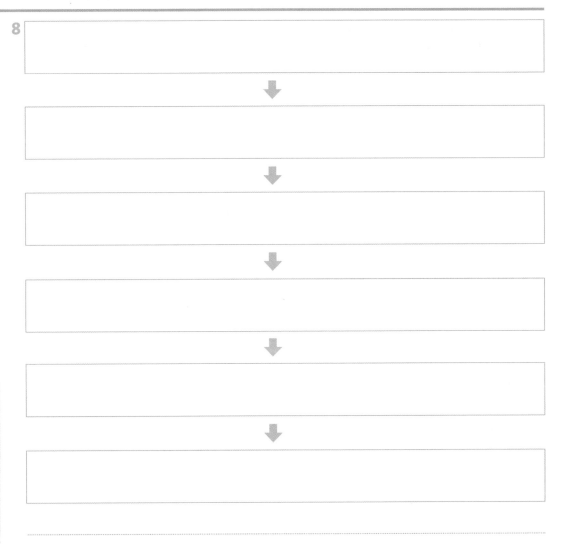

Questions

9 Who was to blame for the hyperinflation of 1923: the French and Belgians; the Weimar government; or the treaty makers at Versailles? Explain your answer.

9
....
....
....
....
....
....

10 Why was the Weimar government more successful in the years 1924–29?

Below is a jumbled list of reasons. Put each point into the most appropriate box in the table.
- Bitter memories of the First World War were beginning to fade
- Young Plan agreed
- Strict pre-war censorship abolished
- Stresemann's leadership (*use twice*)
- New styles reflecting real life became popular
- US loans came through the Dawes Plan

10

Success	Reasons for success
Economic recovery Inflation ended, new more stable currency, full employment, reparations reduced	▪ ▪ ▪
Improved relations with other countries e.g. Locarno Treaties 1925; League of Nations 1926	▪ ▪
Cultural achievements New trends in art, literature and cinema, e.g. antiwar themes	▪ ▪

Questions

11 Describe briefly **three** weaknesses of the Weimer government that remained despite this period of recovery.

11
....
....
....
....
....
....
....

12 The following terms are defined in the table. Write each term next to the correct definition.

- Demilitarisation
- Passive resistance
- Proportional representation
- Coalition government
- Constitution
- Putsch
- Extremist parties
- Inflation
- Armistice
- Reparations

12

Definition	Term
The rules by which a country is governed	
A voting system whereby the number of seats in parliament is in proportion to the number of votes cast in the election	
The agreement to cease the fighting in November 1918	
A government formed by two or more parties	
When a region is kept free of any kind of military forces	
A sum of money to be paid for damage caused in the First World War	
An attempt to seize power by force	
Resisting an enemy using non-violent methods	
When money loses its value and buys less and less	
Political groups willing to use violence to achieve their aims	

Source questions

13 What does Source A tell us about the Spartacist movement in Germany in 1919?

- Explain what *can* be learned about the movement. Do not describe limitations of the source, i.e. what *cannot* be learned.

14 What different impression do you get of the Spartacists from Source B?

- You must explain *how* the sources differ, not why.
- Compare details in both sources. Note differences in *tone* and *language*.

Source A

The Spartacists did not believe the new Parliament would make Germany truly democratic. Rosa Luxemburg believed the new Parliament would give the middle class more power than the working class. She wanted Germany to be ruled instead by 'soviets' — councils made up of workers and soldiers.

From *Germany 1918–1945* by Josh Brooman, 1996 — a history textbook for schools

Source B

The Spartacists are fighting for total power. Where they are in control all personal freedom and security is abolished. Parts of Berlin are the scene of bloody battles. Other parts are without water and light. Food supplies are being stopped. The government is taking all measures necessary to destroy this rule of terror.

From a poster produced by the Weimar government in January 1919

13

14

Questions

15 Why do you think Sources A and B give such different impressions of the Spartacists? Explain your answer using Sources A and B and your own knowledge.
- You must give *reasons* for the differences. Do not repeat *how* the sources differ.
- Think about where the sources come from and the different purposes of the authors.

16 How useful is Source C in explaining the inflationary crisis in Germany in 1923? Use the source and your own knowledge to explain your answer.
- Try to show how the source is useful in some ways but of limited use in other ways.
- Support your argument by referring to the source and by using your knowledge of events linked to the crisis.

15

16

Source C
The price of a loaf of bread in Berlin

Date	Cost in marks
December 1918	0.54
December 1922	163.90
January 1923	250.00
March 1923	463.00
July 1923	3,465.00
September 1923	1,512,000,000.00
November 1923	201,000,000,000,000.00

Questions

Extended writing

On separate paper, write a short essay in answer to the following question.

17 How far had the Weimar Republic succeeded in solving its economic and political problems by the start of 1929?

17

Guidelines

A very good answer will include:

- clearly explained examples of economic and political problems that had been solved
- clearly explained examples of problems that remained
- some attempt to judge the extent to which things were better ('how far…')

Notes

In 1919, Adolf Hitler joined a small, insignificant political group called the German Workers' Party, led by **Anton Drexler**. The party renamed itself the National Socialist German Workers' Party (the NSDAP, or Nazis for short). The NSDAP grew steadily in southern Germany after Hitler became its leader in 1921, mainly because of Hitler's powerful public speaking.

The SA ('Stormtroopers') was created in 1921 as a kind of private army. Members were also known as 'Brownshirts' because of the colour of their uniform. They were to play a key part in Hitler's rise to power from 1930 to 1933.

The Munich Putsch, November 1923

In the second half of 1923, the Weimar government was very unpopular. Hundreds of thousands had suffered as a result of the inflation, and when Stresemann called off the campaign of passive resistance in the Ruhr it seemed to many that this was 'giving in' to the French. Consequently, Hitler felt the time was right to attempt to overthrow the Weimar Republic. He saw it as a weak form of government and held it responsible for Germany's defeat in 1918 and the hated Treaty of Versailles.

In the belief that he had the support of leading conservatives in Bavaria who were also opposed to the Weimar Republic, Hitler planned to seize control of Munich as a first step before going on to Berlin. However, the so-called 'Beer Hall Putsch' in November was a fiasco. The Nazis did not have enough military or popular support and the Bavarian police stopped their march through the city easily.

This failure had serious **short-term** consequences for the Nazi Party. Hitler was imprisoned and the party was temporarily banned, and split into bickering factions. However, in the **long term** Hitler benefited from the putsch:

- At his trial he was allowed to make long speeches and he became well known in Germany.
- It made him rethink his tactics. He decided that the Nazis would have to seek power legally by putting up candidates for election and winning seats in the Reichstag.
- While in prison Hitler wrote *Mein Kampf* ('*My Struggle*'), in which he set out his main beliefs.

The main beliefs of Nazism

These were based on the ideas described in *Mein Kampf* and the 25-point programme drawn up in 1920 by Hitler and Anton Drexler:

- The Aryan race (white northern Europeans) was a '**master race**'. Other races, especially the Jews, were inferior.
- The Treaty of Versailles should be abolished.
- All German-speaking people should be united and Germany's military strength rebuilt.
- Extra living space was needed for Germany's future expansion and this would be found in Poland and Russia.
- Democracy was weak and Germany needed strong central government under one strong leader, a Führer to whom total loyalty would be required.

Hitler rebuilds the National Socialist Party

Hitler had been sentenced to 5 years in prison, but he was released in December 1924. Shortly after, the ban on his party was lifted and, helped by people such as Goebbels and Himmler, he rebuilt it successfully over the following 4 years. New sections were added, such as the Hitler Youth and the **SS** (which, acted at first as a special group of bodyguards to Hitler). However, these were years of economic recovery (see page 6) and the Nazis made little progress in elections. In 1928 they won only 12 seats in the Reichstag.

Economic crisis, 1929–33

October 1929 saw two important events: first the death of Stresemann and then the **Wall Street Crash**, which sparked off a depression in the USA and a reduction in its trade with other countries. This affected Germany especially badly as US banks called in the loans to German banks that had financed recovery in the mid-1920s. This led to the collapse of many businesses in Germany and as unemployment rose, so did support for the Nazis. In 1930 they won 107 seats in the Reichstag; in July 1932 they won 230 seats, although this fell to 196 seats in the November 1932 election. Four main factors helped to increase support for the Nazis at this time.

Economic problems

- Inflation was *not* a problem but unemployment was — 6 million people were out of work by 1932.
- As people became more desperate they were more ready to listen to the Nazis' promises of 'work and bread'.
- To help meet the cost of unemployment benefits the government, under Brüning's leadership, cut the pay of government employees, increased taxes and reduced benefits. This made the government unpopular with those both in work and out of it.

Propaganda and violence

- The SA played an important part in Hitler's campaigns, beating up opponents (mainly socialists and Communists) and attacking their meetings.
- Propaganda posters urged voters to see Hitler as the only way of getting Germany back on its feet and appealed to anti-Semitic feeling by blaming the Jews for all economic problems.

Hitler's political skills

- Hitler was a very effective party leader and campaigner (for example his 'Hitler over Germany' campaign, in which he flew to different cities in the same day).
- He was a powerful public speaker and his mass political meetings won many new supporters.
- He was skilled at putting over simple policies (see page 15), which appealed to different groups within Germany.

Political problems

- The Communists also gained seats after 1929 — this frightened many industrialists, who began to give financial help to the Nazis.
- The other democratic parties failed to agree on how to deal with mass unemployment. This weakened further the faith of many Germans in the democratic parties and the Weimar Republic. It seemed that only Hitler could offer Germany strong, effective leadership.
- In July 1930 President Hindenburg began to help Chancellor Brüning, bypassing the Reichstag and making new laws through his emergency power of 'rule by decree'.

Brüning was dismissed by Hindenburg in May 1932 and was replaced first by **Franz von Papen** and then by **Kurt von Schleicher**. Neither was able to produce the stable government wanted by the 84-year-old Hindenburg and both depended on his use of presidential decrees. As leader of the biggest single party in the Reichstag, Hitler also had a claim to the post of chancellor. He had lost the presidential election to Hindenburg in March 1932 but gained an impressive 13 million votes. Hindenburg disliked Hitler intensely but wanted to appoint a chancellor who would have the support of the Reichstag.

Finally, in January 1933, after a series of secret meetings, von Papen and other conservative politicians persuaded Hindenburg to dismiss von Schleicher and make Hitler chancellor with von Papen as vice-chancellor. The politicians believed they would be able to control him. This came at a time when support for the Nazis was beginning to fall, as shown by the election result of November 1932.

The **short-term** economic and political problems that followed the Wall Street Crash, the skilful campaigns and leadership of Hitler and the use of propaganda and violence all helped to increase support for the Nazis in the period 1930–32. The **long-term** lack of loyalty towards the Weimar Republic because of its association with defeat in the war, the Treaty of Versailles and reparations also contributed. However, Hitler's final step to power was brought about not so much through the mass support of the German people, but through the plans of a small group of scheming politicians.

Questions

Use the information provided, your class notes and your textbook to answer the following questions.

1 Which political party did Hitler join in 1919 and when did he become its leader?

2 Why did Hitler dislike the Weimar Republic?

3 Why did Hitler decide that November 1923 was the right time to try to overthrow this government?

4 Was the Munich Putsch a complete failure for Hitler and the Nazis? Explain your answer.

5 Describe any **three** main beliefs of Nazism.

1

2

3

4

5

Questions

6 Why did the National Socialists win so few seats in the Reichstag from 1924 to 1928?

6

....

....

....

....

7 Complete the timeline opposite by matching the following jumbled events with the correct dates.
- Brüning was dismissed as chancellor
- The Nazis won 196 seats in the Reichstag
- Stresemann died
- Hitler was made chancellor of Germany
- The Wall Street Crash started the Depression
- Hindenburg began to 'rule by decree'
- The Nazis won 230 seats in the Reichstag

7

Date	Event
October 1929	
October 1929	
July 1930	
May 1932	
July 1932	
November 1932	
January 1933	

8 Who were the Brownshirts and how did they help Hitler come to power by 1933?

8

....

....

....

....

....

9 Complete the table opposite by writing in your own notes to explain how the points given in each box helped Hitler come to power in 1933.

Millions became unemployed between 1929 and 1933.	Support for the Communists grew from 1929 to 1933.	The democratic parties failed to work together to find a solution to the unemployment crisis.
This helped Hitler because	This helped Hitler because	This helped Hitler because
Hitler had many political skills.	**Von Papen and other politicians thought they could control Hitler.**	**The Weimar Republic was linked to the hated Treaty of Versailles.**
This helped Hitler because	This helped Hitler because	This helped Hitler because

Questions

Source A

I don't know how to describe the emotions that swept over me as I heard Adolf Hitler. His appeal to German manhood was like a call to arms; the gospel he preached, a sacred truth. I forgot everything but the man. Glancing around me I saw his magnetism as holding these thousands as one.

A Nazi supporter describing his reaction to a speech by Hitler

Source B

Date	Votes in elections for the Nazis	Unemployment in Germany
1928	810,000	1,333,000
1930	6,400,000	3,365,000
July 1932	13,700,000	6,128,000
November 1932	11,700,000	5,900,000

Source questions

10 What does Source A tell us about why people supported Hitler in the early 1930s?

- Explain what can be learned about Hitler's political skills. Do not repeat what the source says but use short quotations to support your answer.

11 How useful is Source B in explaining the increase in popularity of the Nazi Party from 1928 to 1932? Explain your answer using Source B and your own knowledge.

- Try to show how the source is useful in some ways but of limited use in other ways.
- Support your argument by referring to the source and by using your knowledge of other factors that helped to increase the popularity of the Nazis.

10

11

Questions

12 Source C is an interpretation of how Hitler came to power. Do you agree or disagree with this interpretation? Explain your answer using Source C and your own knowledge.

- Consider how you could agree with the interpretation in some ways but disagree in other ways.
- Support your answer by referring to details in Source C, details in other sources and your own knowledge of the factors that helped Hitler gain power in Germany.

Extended writing

On separate paper, write a short essay in answer to the following question.

13 In 1928 there was little support in Germany for the Nazi Party, yet Hitler was made chancellor in January 1933. What happened between 1929 and January 1933 to make this possible?

Use Sources A, B and C above and your own knowledge to explain your answer.

Source C

12

PUNCH CARTOON LIBRARY

A cartoon from an English magazine published soon after Hitler came to power. Hitler is shown being carried on the shoulders of President Hindenburg and von Papen

13

Guidelines

A very good answer will include:

- use of the sources; refer to them separately and by name, e.g. 'Source A shows...'
- use of your knowledge of the period to show that other factors, not shown in the sources, also played a part; explain clearly how at least two of these other factors helped Hitler
- a clear conclusion explaining the factor that you think helped Hitler most or how his success was the result of different factors working together

Germany did not become a dictatorship in January 1933. Hitler was head of a **coalition government**: nine of the twelve men in his first cabinet were not Nazis.

From democracy to dictatorship: January 1933–August 1934

The coalition did not have a majority in the Reichstag and Hindenburg still had the power to dismiss Hitler at any time. To change all this, Hitler first needed to increase his own powers through an Enabling Law. As this would involve a change in the constitution, Hitler needed a two-thirds majority in the Reichstag:

- He called an election for March 1933, hoping to increase the number of Nazi seats.
- The **Reichstag Fire** on 27 February gave Hitler the chance to raise fears of a Communist revolution. It is still not clear exactly how the fire was started, but a young Communist was blamed for it. Hitler then persuaded Hindenburg to issue a decree that suspended civil liberties and enabled Hitler to arrest leaders of the Communist Party. In the election of 5 March the Nazis won 288 seats, but Hitler still did not have the majority he needed.

However, Hitler persuaded the Reichstag to pass the **Enabling Law**, which gave him the power to make laws for the next 4 years without consulting Parliament. Only the Social Democrats voted against this. The 81 Communist MPs, who would also have opposed it, were banned from serving in the Reichstag by Hindenburg at Hitler's request. Intimidation and threats of violence by the SA, who crowded the galleries during the debate, may have encouraged some people to abstain or support the Enabling Law against their real wishes.

Bringing Germany into line

Hitler now used his new powers to 'bring Germany into line'. A series of laws was passed which put every aspect of German life under the control of the Nazis:

- On 2 May 1933, trade union officials all over the country were arrested and all trade unions combined in the **German Labour Front** with a Nazi at its head.
- On 10 May, books by Jews or anyone whose ideas were disapproved of were burned publicly.
- During May and June 1933 all other political parties in Germany were closed down and their leaders arrested. By July the Nazi Party was the only legal party in Germany.

Two problems remained:

- **The SA and its leader, Ernst Röhm**. The SA played a large part in helping Hitler come to power from 1929 to 1933, but continued street violence by members was now an embarrassment. Moreover, Röhm was becoming more ambitious for himself. SA numbers had reached 4 million by June 1934 and there was talk of a merger of the army and SA — with Röhm at its head. Army chiefs were alarmed at this and Hitler decided to act. On the **Night of the Long Knives** (30 June 1934) **SS** squads arrested and murdered Röhm and over 300 other SA leaders. In one night Hitler had not only removed a growing threat to his own power, but also gained the support of the army.

- **Hindenburg**. He was still president and could, in theory, dismiss Hitler. When he died on 2 August 1934, Hitler combined the offices of president and chancellor, making himself **Führer** (leader) of Germany. The following day all soldiers in Germany swore an **oath** of personal loyalty to Hitler. He was now in total control.

Why was it so easy to create the dictatorship?

It was very difficult for opponents to stop it.

- Following the Enabling Law, everything the Nazis did was legal.
- People who might have led opposition — the leaders of political parties and trade unions — were sent to **concentration camps**, together with anyone else who dared speak out against Hitler. At first the camps were just quickly erected prison camps in which prisoners suffered harsh treatment and were forced to do hard labour. Much worse was to come later.
- Democracy had never been embraced fully in Weimar Germany, especially by conservatives in the landowning and business classes, and its passing was not widely mourned.

The totalitarian state, 1934–39

After August 1934 Hitler aimed to turn Germany into a totalitarian state — one in which the government had total control over all aspects of life and individual rights and freedoms did not exist. This was achieved through the creation of a police state.

There were two main instruments of this police state:

- **The Gestapo (secret state police)**. This was commanded by **Reinhard Heydrich**. Gestapo agents could arrest people and send them to concentration camps without trial. Fear of the Gestapo turned Germany into a nation of informers as people tried to protect themselves by incriminating others.
- **The SS**. Run by **Heinrich Himmler**, the SS also existed to seek out potential enemies of the Nazi state and had unlimited power. Two important subdivisions of the SS were the **Death's Head Units**, which were to run the concentration camps, and the **Waffen SS**, which fought alongside the regular army in the Second World War.

Why was there so little opposition to the Nazis from 1934 to 1939?

- **Censorship** of the radio and newspapers meant opposing views were never published.
- Organisations such as political parties and trade unions, which might have led opposition effectively, ceased to exist after the summer of 1933.
- **Fear** of the Gestapo and SS kept people quiet.

However, many Germans had no wish to oppose the Nazis:

- The economic recovery between 1934 and 1939 reduced unemployment greatly (see Topic 4).
- In foreign affairs Germany seemed to have regained its status as a world power and had put right the humiliations inflicted by the Treaty of Versailles (e.g. by building up the armed forces, remilitarising the Rhineland in 1936 and uniting with Austria in 1938).

Consequently, Hitler was genuinely popular and seen as a strong, successful leader whose achievements compensated for the loss of many rights and freedoms.

Opposition, 1939–45

The outbreak of the Second World War changed this state of affairs. After 1942, when things started to go badly for Germany, opposition groups did begin to appear. They opposed the Nazis in different ways and for different reasons.

- **The White Rose movement**. Hans and Sophie Scholl were students at Munich University in the early war years. Disillusion-ment with war and horror at the mass murder of Polish Jews led them to form, with other students, a group called the 'White Rose' (used as a password and symbol of Christian love). Throughout 1942 they produced and circulated leaflets encouraging the use of passive resistance against the German war effort and daubed anti-Nazi slogans on walls. Hans and Sophie were eventually caught and both were executed by guillotine in February 1943. The square where the central hall of Munich University is located has been named 'Geschwister-Scholl-Platz' in their memory.

- **Communist groups**. These aimed to help Russia defeat Germany by carrying out acts of sabotage and distributing propaganda leaflets to factory workers in the hope of encouraging strikes. One small group, **Red Orchestra**, operated a spy network which passed military information to the Russians.

- **The Kreisau Circle**. This was a group of aristocrats, intellectuals and professional people who held secret meetings in the town of Kreisau. They hated the dictatorship and planned a democratic form of government which could be put in place if Hitler was overthrown. Some of their members were involved in the attempt to seize power in July 1944.

- **The July Bomb Plot, 1944**. This was a plan, organised by a group of army officers and government officials, to assassinate Hitler and take control of the government. The plotters were convinced that Germany was losing the war and that Hitler was leading the country to disaster. An army officer, **Count Claus von Stauffenberg**, planted a bomb in Hitler's conference room but Hitler survived the explosion, suffering only minor injuries. Revenge against the conspirators was swift and brutal and up to 5,000 people died in the following weeks.

- **Jehovah's Witnesses**. They resisted by refusing, for religious reasons, to give the Nazi salute or to join the German army. Many were sent to concentration camps and nearly 2,000 died as a result of Nazi persecution.

- **The Edelweiss Pirates**. See Topic 6 for details.

All these groups worked separately from one another and this inevitably weakened their efforts. Cooperation in a police state, at a time of war, would have been impossible. Many ordinary Germans resisted in their own individual ways, for example by telling anti-Nazi jokes or by sheltering Jews. Around 800,000 people were arrested for some form of resistance and of these, only approximately 300,000 were still alive in 1945.

Questions

Use the information provided, your class notes and your textbook to answer the following questions.

1 Complete the timeline by matching the following jumbled events with the correct dates.
- The Enabling Law was passed
- The National Socialist Party was the only legal party
- The Reichstag burned down
- Books the Nazis disapproved of were burned
- President Hindenburg died
- Hitler became chancellor
- The Night of the Long Knives
- The last democratic election was held
- The German Labour Front replaced all trade unions

2 Why was Hitler not satisfied with his position as chancellor of Germany?

3 What power did the Enabling Law give to Hitler?

4 Why had the SA become a problem for Hitler by 1934?

5 What happened on the Night of the Long Knives?

Date	Event
January 1933	
February 1933	
March 1933	
March 1933	
May 1933	
May 1933	
July 1933	
June 1934	
August 1934	

2

3

4

5

Questions

6 Complete the table opposite by explaining how each of the following events helped Hitler build a dictatorship in Germany from February 1933 to June 1934:

- the Reichstag Fire
- the Enabling Law
- the Night of the Long Knives
- the death of Hindenburg

6

Event	How it helped establish the dictatorship
The Reichstag Fire	
The Enabling Law	
The Night of the Long Knives	
The death of Hindenburg	

7 Give **two** reasons that explain why Hitler was able to change Germany from a democracy to a dictatorship so easily.

7

8 What is meant by the term 'totalitarian state'?

8

Questions

9 Explain briefly how the following organisations helped give the government total control over the German people:
 a the Gestapo
 b the SS

9a ....

....

b ....

....

10 Complete the table by adding your own notes in the spaces provided.

Groups who opposed the Nazis	Why they opposed them	How they opposed them
Edelweiss Pirates (see Topic 6 for details)		
White Rose		
Red Orchestra		
Kreisau Circle		
Army officers		
Jehovah's Witnesses		

Questions

Source A

I swear by God this holy oath: I will render unconditional obedience to the Führer of the German Reich and People, Adolf Hitler, the Supreme Commander of the Armed Forces.

An oath taken by all soldiers of the German Army, August 1934

Source questions

11 What can you learn from Sources A and B about how the Nazis established control over Germany after Hitler came to power? Use details from the sources in your answer.
- You must refer to details in both sources in your answer.

12 How useful is Source C in explaining how the Nazis prevented opposition in Germany? Use the source and your own knowledge to explain your answer.
- Try to show how the source is useful in some ways but of limited use in other ways.
- Support your argument by referring to the source and by using your knowledge of other methods used by the Nazis to prevent opposition.

Source B

Anyone who discusses politics, carries on controversial talks and meetings or loiters around with others will be hanged.

From the regulations at Dachau concentration camp, 1933. Quoted in *Weimar and Nazi Germany* by S. Lee, 1996

11

12

Source C
Members of the SA burning books, 10 May 1933

Source D

We were living in great times and their creator and guarantor was Hitler. Adolf Hitler, for us, was the impressive Führer figure. We awaited each speech with the tingling expectation that he was about to announce a new German success. We were seldom disappointed.

A German looking back on his life in the late 1930s. Quoted in *Hitler's Domestic Policy* by A. Boxer, 1997

13 How does Source D help us understand why there was so little opposition to the Nazis up until 1939? Use the source and your own knowledge to explain your answer.
- Use your knowledge to give examples of the kind of 'success' referred to in the source.
- Explain how this helped prevent opposition.

13

....

....

....

....

....

....

Extended writing

On separate paper, write a short essay in answer to the following question.

14 'The reason why the Nazis faced so little opposition from 1934 to 1939 was simple — it was terror!' How far do you agree with this statement? Use Sources A–D above and your own knowledge to explain your answer.

14

Guidelines
A very good answer will include explanations supported by:
- references to at least **three** named sources
- knowledge of other reasons for the lack of opposition not shown in the sources
- a clear, supported conclusion that tries to assess the extent to which the statement is true

Hitler had three main aims in the period up to 1936:
- to reduce unemployment
- to rebuild Germany's military strength
- to develop control over all aspects of the economy

After 1936 his priority was to prepare for war.

1933–36

The first two of the aims listed above were achieved through:
- **Public works**. Projects such as building new homes and planting forests created further employment. One of the most successful of these projects was the building of a network of motorways (**autobahns**) across Germany — over 3,000 kilometres of them between 1933 and 1938. Some of this work was carried out by members of the **National Labour Service (RAD)**, which was introduced for all 18–25-year-olds and run along military lines. It involved doing manual labour, on low pay, for 6 months and provided elements of political indoctrination and preparation for the army.
- **Rearmament**. This created vast numbers of new jobs in the factories making guns, aeroplanes and shells. It also stimulated other industries such as iron and steel production.
- **Conscription**. This was introduced in 1935 to build up numbers in the armed forces and reduce unemployment figures.

Nazi control of the economy

This brought disadvantages as well as benefits. All trade unions were abolished and workers had to join the **DAF** (*Deutsche Arbeitsfront* — German Labour Front), run by the Nazi Robert Ley. This placed the workers under total control. They could not negotiate for better pay or even move from job to job freely. Wages were low and working hours were long.

However, the Nazis also wanted to create a 'people's community' in which differences between the social classes would disappear. Therefore, within the DAF, two special organisations were set up:
- The **KdF** (*Kraft durch Freude* — 'Strength through Joy') scheme provided benefits for workers such as cheap sea cruises, coach tours, theatre visits and sports facilities. This opened up new leisure opportunities previously unavailable to low-paid workers and was very successful, although it was mostly loyal party workers who benefited. One particularly popular KdF scheme aimed to provide workers with a **Volkswagen** ('people's car'). Thousands paid instalments of 5 marks a week in order to secure their car, but in 1940 the factory switched to war production and no one actually received one.
- The **Beauty of Labour** scheme aimed to improve working conditions through, for example, better ventilation and lighting and the provision of good, cheap meals in works canteens.

These schemes had the additional purpose of compensating workers for their loss of rights and keeping them content.

The rebuilding of Germany's economic strength during this period was in the hands of the financial expert **Dr Hjalmar Schacht**, who was made minister of the economy in 1934 and given wide powers. Schacht was not, however, in favour of the significant change in policy that came in 1936: Hitler ordered that the German economy be made ready for war within 4 years. Schacht argued that Germany could not afford both to raise the standard of living and to continue building up the armed forces, so he resigned in 1937.

The Four-Year Plan, 1936–40: preparing for war

Hermann Goering, head of the German air force, was in charge of the Four-Year Plan, a key element of which was to make Germany self-sufficient in the production of food and raw materials — a policy known as **autarky**. In the First World War Germany had been starved of vital supplies for its industries by the British naval blockade. Hitler wanted his scientists and industrialists to find substitutes for materials such as oil and rubber so that Germany would not be dependent on foreign imports.

For ordinary people this often meant that consumer goods and even basic foods were in short supply. People were expected to make sacrifices for the national good. As Goering put it, 'Guns make us powerful. Butter only makes us fat.'

Were the Nazis' economic policies successful?

- **Reducing unemployment**. This fell from over 5 million in 1933 to around 0.5 million by 1939 — Nazi policies were successful here.
- **Total control of the economy**. In this respect also, the Nazis were successful. Strikes and industrial disputes were eliminated completely; the government had full control over wages, prices,

imports and distribution of raw materials; even large companies had to change what they produced if the government ordered it.
- **Readiness for war**. The policy of autarky was not successful and in 1939 German imports were still as high as its exports. Despite this, the achievements of the German armed forces in the first 2 years of the Second World War seem to suggest that the German economy was ready for a *short* war, but their eventual defeat in 1945 shows that this policy failed in the *long term*. (See details on the impact of the Second World War on page 33.)

Did the German people really benefit from the policies to 1939?

- **Working-class** people lost all their trade union rights and had to work long hours for low pay. Wages hardly rose at all during the 1930s. However, the KdF scheme was popular and most people remembered the misery of the depression years, 1929–33. Working life under the Nazis may have been hard, but at least the workers had jobs again.
- The fortunes of the **middle classes** were similarly mixed. They were pleased to see order and calm restored to the streets and the threat of communism dealt with. However, shopkeepers and owners of small businesses struggled to make a good living. People did not have enough spare cash to buy **consumer goods** (non-essential goods for the home such as electrical goods) and although the Nazis passed laws to ban new department stores, existing ones provided stiff competition for small businesses.
- Those who gained most were the **owners of large companies**, especially those involved in the armaments industries. They no longer had to deal with troublesome trade unions, the wages of

workers were kept firmly under control and huge profits were made from government contracts. However, there were occasions when the government interfered with the running of their businesses, for example when factories were ordered to switch production to other goods. This happened more frequently when Germany was preparing for war.

All social classes shared the greater sense of national pride that developed in the late 1930s — pride in the new buildings that improved the appearance of towns and cities, in the new motorways across the country and in the rebuilding of their armed forces.

The impact of war on the economy

Military successes from September 1939 to the end of 1941 give the impression that Germany was well-prepared for war. However, by 1942 Germany was fighting Russia and the USA as well as Britain. The demands of a long world war were becoming a massive drain on the economy. **Albert Speer** was made minister of armaments in 1942 and under his leadership war production was stepped up, reaching a peak in the summer of 1944. This effort could not be sustained and Germany's economy weakened in line with the deterioration of its military situation in the last year of the war.

Life for German civilians also deteriorated:

- Allied bombing raids on German cities increased from 1942, reaching a climax with a massive raid on **Dresden** in February 1945 which killed between 35,000 and 150,000 people in just 2 days.
- There were increasing food shortages.
- Refugees fleeing from Russian forces were advancing from the east.

By April 1945 Berlin, the centre of Hitler's empire, was in ruins.

Questions

Use the information provided, your class notes and your textbook to answer the following questions.

1 What were Hitler's **three** main aims for the German economy up to 1936?

2 Describe **three** things that were done to reduce unemployment.

3 What became the main priority for the German economy from 1936 onwards?

4 Complete the table by writing each term from the list below next to the correct description.
- Beauty of Labour
- Autarky
- RAD
- KdF
- DAF
- Consumer goods

1

2

3

4

Description	Term
Involved 6 months' compulsory labour service for 18–25-year-olds	
A Nazi-run organisation that replaced all trade unions	
Organised cheap holidays and leisure activities for low-paid workers	
A policy that aimed to make Germany self-sufficient	
Non-essential goods for the home, e.g. electrical goods	
Organised ways of improving working conditions	

Questions

5 Why was the DAF (German Labour Front) set up to replace trade unions?

6 What was the role of Dr Schacht in the German government?

7 What did Goering mean when he said: 'Guns make us powerful. Butter only makes us fat'?

8 Why could the Nazis claim success by 1939 in:
a reducing unemployment?
b gaining total control over the economy?

9 What reasons did the Nazis have for introducing schemes such as Beauty of Labour and the KdF?

5

6

7

8a

b

9

10 Were the German people better off as a result of the Nazis' economic policies? Complete the table by writing your own notes in the spaces provided.

Social group	Better off in these respects	Worse off in these respects
Working class		
Middle class/owners of small businesses		
Owners of large companies		

11 In what sense were people in all social classes pleased with Nazi economic policies up to 1939?

11

....

....

....

Questions

12 Describe the impact of the Second World
War on:
a the German economy
b German civilians

12a

....
....
....
....

b

....
....
....
....

> ### Source A
> Special mention here should be made of a part of the German
> Labour Front called 'Strength through Joy'...The section for travel-
> ling and hiking is perhaps the most popular one...Its pleasure
> cruises to foreign countries have attracted great attention. Equally
> valuable have been tours within Germany. In 1934 some 2 million
> Germans had taken part, by 1936 — 6 million.
>
> An extract from *Germany Speaks*, written in the 1930s by Robert Ley. Quoted in
> *Nazi Power in Germany* by Greg and Jean Thie, 1989

Source questions

13 What does Source A suggest about the
effectiveness of KdF?
- What overall impression do you get of
  the effectiveness of this organisation?
- Quote details from the source to
  support your answer.

13

....
....
....
....

Source B

Subsidised holidays and leisure pursuits were available but most workers could not afford the most desirable KdF benefits. Nazi efforts to bring all Germans together in a 'people's community' had more to do with propaganda than reality.

From *Hitler's Domestic Policy* by A. Boxer, 1997 — a textbook for secondary schools

14 What different view do you get of the effectiveness of KdF from Source B?
- You must compare Sources A and B, saying how they differ. Quote details from both.
- Explain how the overall impressions of the two sources differ.

14

15 Why do you think that Sources A and B give different views of the effectiveness of KdF?
- You must explain why they differ, so think about differences in author, intended audience and publication date.

15

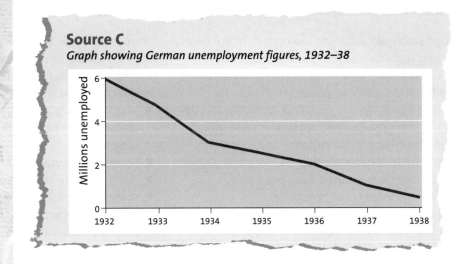

Source C
Graph showing German unemployment figures, 1932–38

16 How useful is Source C for judging the success of Nazi economic policies up until 1938? Use the source and your own knowledge to explain your answer.
- Use details in the source to explain how it is useful.
- Use your knowledge of other policies to explain the limitations of this source.

16

Extended writing

On separate paper, write a short essay in answer to the following question.

17 Did the Nazis really improve the lives of German workers between 1933 and 1939?

17

You could include the following in your answer and any other information of your own:
- Forty per cent of all factory workers were unemployed in 1932.
- All workers belonged to the DAF (German Labour Front).
- Cheap leisure activities were made available to workers.

Women in Weimar Germany enjoyed improved opportunities: they had the right to vote and were able to join professions such as medicine and law on an equal basis with men. This new status declined rapidly after the Nazis came to power:

- The numbers of women employed in teaching, medicine and the civil service were reduced greatly. Male applicants were given preference over females where qualifications were equal. Women in top jobs in these areas were sacked.
- Female lawyers and judges were barred from practising.
- Only 10% of university students could be female.
- Women were stopped from serving on juries as it was felt that they were affected too much by their emotions and unable to think logically.

The role of women in Nazi society

For the Nazis, the role of women in society was to look after their homes, their husbands and, most importantly, to have lots of children, preferably boys — a vision summed up by the 'Three Ks' — '**Kinder, Küche und Kirche**' ('Children, Kitchen and Church'). This attitude was partly the result of what we would call today the sexist assumption that it was natural for the male to be the worker and provider while the female's place was in the home.

Germany's birth rate was falling and this had to be reversed in order to provide more soldiers for the army in the future. Removing women from the workplace would also help reduce the severe unemployment of the early 1930s. Consequently, policies were introduced to encourage marriage, raise the status of motherhood and increase the number of births:

- Marriage loans were given to brides who gave up their jobs, and a quarter of the repayment was cancelled for each child they had.
- Family allowances were introduced for low-paid workers.
- 'Mothers' Day' became an annual national holiday in May 1934.
- A special medal was introduced — the '**Honour Cross of the German Mother**' — which was awarded to especially fertile mothers: a bronze medal for four or five children, silver for six or seven and gold for eight or more.

In addition to this, abortion was made illegal and contraceptives were made more difficult to obtain.

Producing healthy and 'racially pure' children

Welfare schemes were introduced to ensure the development of healthy children:

- Local Nazi organisations distributed milk, grocery parcels and baby clothes.
- A special organisation, the **Deutsches Frauenwerk** (German Women's Enterprise), set up mothercraft and housecraft lessons for newly-married women. Some were able to attend special **bridal schools** set up to create perfect mothers and wives. Here, 6-week courses were offered teaching cookery, baby care and

thrifty housekeeping, with a special diploma at the end for 'master housewives'.

- After 1939, childcare facilities for working mothers were improved.

Infant mortality (deaths of children in the first year of life) was reduced in the 1930s, possibly as a result of these policies. However, the Nazis wanted not just greater numbers of births, but children of the 'right' quality.

- A compulsory **sterilisation** programme was introduced in July 1933 to prevent women who were deemed 'unfit' (e.g. those with hereditary diseases or suffering from mental illness) from having children. By 1939 over 350,000 women had been sterilised forcibly.
- From 1935 a **Marriage Law** required a certificate of 'fitness to marry' (i.e. proof of 'racial and medical purity') before a licence could be issued. The future wives of SS members were subjected to especially detailed investigations going back several generations.
- The **Lebensborn** ('Spring of Life') programme, introduced by SS leader Heinrich Himmler in 1935, set up homes to look after orphaned and illegitimate children of 'racially sound' Germans. Selected unmarried women were encouraged to 'donate a baby to the Führer' by having children by SS officers. By 1944 nearly 11,000 children had been born because of this programme.

Women's behaviour and appearance

The Nazis also aimed to control the appearance and behaviour of women. Propaganda posters usually portrayed an idealised woman with blonde hair, either covered by a peasant-style headscarf or in plaits or a bun, with no make-up and wearing a full skirt. Pressure was put on women not to smoke and to avoid wearing clothes made of imported wool, silk or cotton.

How did German women react to Nazi policies towards them?

It is difficult to know how women reacted to these policies as open criticism of them would have been both difficult and dangerous. It is likely that those professional women whose jobs in medicine and the civil service were taken away from them, resented this. On the other hand, some historians have argued that:

- The development of women's organisations and youth groups such as the League of German Maidens (see page 51) gave women increased opportunities to become involved in public life.
- Some women accepted Nazi ideas fully and took pride in their status as mothers.
- In small towns and rural areas, traditional ideas about the role of women would have been strong to begin with, so Nazi views may have simply reinforced these.

Throughout the period 1933–45 no women held positions of importance within the Nazi Party. Two women who did achieve public prominence were:

- **Gertrude Scholtz-Klink** became head of the different Nazi women's organisations in 1934. She represented the ideal Nazi woman in many respects since she was blonde, healthy, a mother to four children and a total supporter of all the party's aims. In reality she had little political power since major decisions were made by her male superiors.

- **Leni Riefenstahl** was a film director who achieved national and international acclaim for her films of the Nuremberg Rally of 1934 (*Triumph of the Will*) and of the 1936 Olympic Games (*Olympia*).

Were Nazi policies towards women successful?

The policies were partially successful:

- The birth rate did rise between 1933 and 1939 and at a faster rate than in Britain or France, but this could have been the result of lower unemployment. Most couples continued to limit their families to two or three children.
- The marriage rate increased at first but levelled off after 1935.
- The divorce rate continued to be high, partly because divorce was made easier to obtain. For example, childless marriages could be ended because they did not serve the nation's needs.
- The number of women in employment fell from over 7 million in 1928 to 5.7 million by 1936 — but began to rise again after 1937. By 1939 there were more women in work than in 1933.

The effects of rearmament and war

The year 1937 marked a significant change in Nazi policy. By then rearmament and the economic recovery were beginning to create a shortage of male labour and so more women were needed in the workplace. A '**duty year**' was introduced, which encouraged women to take up farm work or help out in a family home without pay.

When the war began in 1939, some Nazi leaders wanted the conscription of women into the workforce. Hitler refused to do this, possibly because it went against his beliefs about the role of women in society. By 1942 more and more women were needed to support the war effort by working in factories, hospitals and on the land and so women were obliged to register for war work.

The Nazis and religion

Before 1933, many Christians supported certain policies of the Nazis, such as:

- their criticism of the decadence of the Berlin nightlife
- the importance they seemed to attach to the family
- their determination to crush communism — an anti-religious political philosophy

Although the Nazis had no interest in the beliefs and values of the Christian Churches, they could not ignore them. Germany was a Christian country: roughly two thirds of its population was Protestant and one third was Catholic. Hitler's aim was, therefore, first to control the Christian Churches, then to reduce their influence gradually before, finally, replacing them.

Relations with the Protestants

In order to control them more easily, the different Protestant Churches were united into one **German Christian Church** under the leadership of a Nazi, Reich Bishop **Ludwig Müller**. He declared his support publicly for all Nazi policies and tried to Nazify the Church, for example by ordering that all church services should begin and end with the Hitler salute.

This attempt to unify and control Protestant Churches failed because hundreds of pastors rejected the German Christians and joined the **Confessional Church** instead, which was led by **Martin Niemöller**, a former First World War submarine commander.

Relations with the Catholic Church

In July 1933 a **concordat** (agreement) was signed in which the Pope promised that Catholic priests would not criticise Nazi policies and Hitler promised not to interfere in Church affairs or with Church schools.

The Nazis did not keep to this agreement and by 1936 they were actively trying to reduce the influence of the Church by discouraging young people from attending Church schools or youth movements. Religious education in state schools was phased out and by 1939 nearly all Church schools had been closed.

Did the Christian Churches actively oppose the Nazis?

There was never any organised criticism of Nazi policies by the Christian Churches. However, individuals within the Churches did speak out and hundreds ended up in concentration camps as a result. The following prominent individuals spoke out against the Nazis:

- **Martin Niemöller** spoke out in sermons against the attempts of the German Christians to Nazify the Protestant faith. He was arrested in 1937 and imprisoned in a concentration camp, where he remained until his release in 1945.
- **Dietrich Bonhöffer**, another member of the Confessional Church, encouraged trainee pastors to resist Nazism before his

college was closed in 1940. During the Second World War he continued to work against the Nazis until his arrest in 1943. He was executed in 1945.

- **Pope Pius XI**, having agreed to the 1933 concordat, became angered by the Nazis' failure to honour their side of the agreement. In 1937 he issued an **encyclical** (letter of importance) condemning all Nazi beliefs and practices as unchristian. This was read from the pulpits of all Catholic churches in Germany. Pius XI died in 1939. His successor, Pius XII, has often been criticised for his failure to speak out against the Nazi treatment of the Jews and other groups during the Second World War.
- In 1941 **Clemens von Galen**, the Catholic Bishop of Münster, attacked the Nazi programme of euthanasia publicly (see page 65 for details of this programme). As a result, this programme was halted temporarily. No action was taken against him for fear of upsetting public opinion, which shows that even by 1941 the Nazis had not succeeded in destroying the influence of the Church.

The German Faith Movement

The German Faith Movement was the kind of faith the Nazis hoped would finally replace Christianity in Germany. It was a pro-Nazi, non-Christian movement based on pagan ceremonies. It had little popular support.

The fact that Christian churches remained open and services continued throughout the Nazi era shows that Hitler ultimately failed in his attempt to destroy Christianity in Germany.

Questions

Use the information provided, your class notes and textbook to answer the following questions.

1 Describe two **steps** the Nazis took after 1933 to reduce the number of women in paid employment.

2 Explain **three** reasons the Nazis had for reducing the number of women in work.

3 Describe **one** method the Nazis used to:
   a encourage early marriage
   b increase the birth rate
   c raise the status of motherhood

4 Describe **three** steps the Nazis took to ensure the development of healthy babies.

5 Explain **two** steps taken to ensure that babies born were 'racially and medically pure'.

6 What image of the ideal woman was presented in Nazi propaganda posters?

1

2

3a

b

c

4

5

6

Questions

7 Did German women welcome Nazi policies towards them? Explain your answer.

7

8 How successful were Nazi policies towards women? Complete the table using your own notes.

8

Policy	Evidence of success	Evidence of limited success/failure
To increase the birth rate		
To encourage marriage		
To reduce the number of women in work		
To produce healthy babies		

9 Explain the changes in Nazi policy towards women that occurred in:
  a 1937
  b 1942

9a

b

Questions

Topic 5 Women and the Church, 1933–45

10 Explain the terms in the table in relation to Nazi views on the role of women in society.

Term	Explanation
'Kinder, Küche und Kirche' (Children, Kitchen and Church)	
Honour Cross of the German Mother	
Bridal schools	
Lebensborn ('Spring of Life') programme	

11 Why did some Christians in Germany support the Nazis?

12 What were Hitler's aims with regard to the Christian Churches?

13 Describe the different ways in which Hitler tried to control:
a the Protestant Churches
b the Catholic Church

13a

Questions

14 Complete the table to show how some Christians tried to resist the Nazis.

	Why they resisted	How they resisted	What happened to them
Martin Niemöller			
Pope Pius XI			
Bishop Galen			
Dietrich Bonhöffer			
Jehovah's Witnesses (see page 25)			

15 What was the German Faith Movement?

15 ....

....

....

Source questions

Source A

Woman has the task of being beautiful and bringing children into the world and this is by no means as old fashioned as one might think. The female bird preens herself for her mate and hatches her eggs for him.

Dr Goebbels, Nazi propaganda chief. Quoted in *Nazi Power in Germany* by Greg and Jean Thie, 1989

16 What does Source A tell us about Nazi views on the role of women in society?
- Do not just describe what the source says. What can be *inferred/deduced* from it?

17 Why would the Nazis have approved of the painting of the family in Source B? Use the source and your own knowledge to explain your answer.
- Think about the hidden messages in this painting.
- Support your answer with reference to details in the picture and your knowledge of what the Nazis wanted from the family.

Source B
'The Family', an oil painting by Wolf Willrich

MARY EVANS PICTURE LIBRARY

16

17

Questions

18 How useful is Source C in explaining Nazi ideas about the role of women in society? Use the source and your own knowledge to explain your answer.

- Try to show how the source is useful in some ways but of limited use in other ways.
- Support your argument by referring to the source and by using your knowledge of how Nazi policies changed over time.

Source C
A poster from 1939 calling on women and girls to help German Rail

18

Extended writing

On separate paper, write a short essay in answer to the following question.

19 How successful were Nazi policies towards women in the period 1933–45? Use Sources A, B and C and your own knowledge to explain your answer.

19

Guidelines

A very good answer will include:

- explanations of what the Nazis aimed to achieve by their policies
- explanations of the extent to which they were successful with each aim
- use of the sources and your knowledge of how their policies changed over the period

Topic 6 — Education and youth movements, 1933–45

The Nazis knew that they would never win over those sections of the population that had never supported them but, if they could control the minds of each new generation, Nazism really could last for 1,000 years. Their policies towards young people had, therefore, one overall aim — to ensure that they developed into loyal, unquestioning supporters of Nazi ideas. This broad aim was to be achieved as follows:

- First, through establishing control of the education system and all youth movements.
- Second, through a process of indoctrination (one-sided education where only Nazi beliefs would be taught) from a very early age.

Education

Control of the education system began in 1933 with the setting up of:

- the Ministry of Education in Berlin, which took responsibility for schools in Germany away from state governments
- a Nazi Teachers' League, which all teachers were expected to join; Jews and teachers who were clearly not committed to Nazi ideas were sacked

Indoctrination within the schools was to be achieved through the rewriting of textbooks to fit in with Nazism and adjustments to the subjects taught. For example:

- In history, pupils learned about past German heroes, about the development of National Socialism and about the injustices of the Treaty of Versailles.

- In biology they learned of the superiority of the Aryan racial type and the need to keep the race pure.
- In mathematics they did calculations that would be useful in a military context.
- Physical education was taught for 2 hours each day. This was especially important to prepare boys for being fit soldiers and girls for being healthy mothers.
- In all subjects no opportunity was missed to teach children that Jewish people belonged to an inferior race and were their enemies.

The Nazis favoured single-sex schools and put more emphasis in the curriculum of girls' schools on domestic science and **eugenics** (the study of how to produce perfect offspring), in keeping with their perceived role in society.

Special institutions were set up for children and young people showing leadership potential:

- **Napolas** (National Political Institutes of Education) for 10–18-year-olds; these 21 schools were run by the SS
- three **Adolf Hitler Schools** for 12–18-year-olds
- **Ordensburgen** (Castles of Knightly Orders) for young men who had completed military service

In these special institutions, and other schools, academic education was given little importance and the emphasis was on physical and military training. As the status of academic subjects fell, so did the numbers of young people going on to higher education. Declining standards also led, after 1939, to labour shortages in technical areas of war production.

Youth movements

The Nazis were not content with just controlling what young people learned in school. The process of indoctrination into Nazism had to continue in the evenings and at the weekend. This was the main purpose of the Hitler Youth movement, first created in 1926 but expanded greatly after 1933.

The organisation of the movement, under the leadership of **Baldur von Schirach**, is shown below.

German name	English equivalent	Gender	Age range
Pimpfen	Cubs or Little Fellows	Boys	6–10
Deutsche Jungvolk (DJ)	German Young People	Boys	10–14
Hitlerjugend (HJ)	Hitler Youth	Boys	14–18
Jungmädel (JM)	Young Girls	Girls	10–14
Bund Deutscher Mädel (BDM)	League of German Girls	Girls	14–17

Government control over young people's lives did not end at 18. Boys had to do 6 months' compulsory service in the RAD (National Labour Service — see page 31) and national service in the army.

Activities

The activities organised by the youth groups included weekend outings to youth hostels, camping and hiking, athletics, political lectures and military games. Through these activities young people were expected to develop skills, values and ideas that the Nazis thought important — such as teamwork, courage, strength, physical fitness, loyalty to Hitler and unquestioning obedience. Summer camps gave poor children the chance of a holiday and they were treated the same as those from more wealthy homes.

Girls' organisations were considered less important, although they included very similar activities apart from military games. **Jutta Rüdiger**, leader of the BDM, described its aim as 'to achieve health, self-discipline, courage and later, through gymnastics, gracefulness'.

Activities sometimes took up several evenings a week and whole weekends. By taking young people away from their parents so frequently it was hoped that the influence of the home would be reduced. HJ members were even encouraged to report their parents for comments or behaviour considered disloyal to the Führer.

Were Nazi policies towards young people successful?

There is no doubt that the Nazis controlled the education system and youth organisations in Germany totally. However, it is more difficult to judge the extent to which they were able to indoctrinate young Germans into Nazism. Accounts written by individuals who grew up during this era give conflicting pictures.

- Some stress the sense of comradeship found in the youth groups, the feeling that they were involved in something relevant and important, and the loyalty they developed for their Führer.
- Others describe the enjoyment of sporting and camping activities but the boredom of political lectures.

Membership of the Hitler Youth certainly grew rapidly — from 108,000 in 1932 to 3,500,000 by 1934 and up to 8 million by 1938. However, being a member did not necessarily mean that a young German was an enthusiastic young Nazi or even that he or she attended meetings. The fact that membership was made **compulsory** in 1939 suggests that for many young people, the Hitler Youth was becoming far less attractive than previously. Some young people went further and resisted more actively.

Youth opposition

Some young people resisted — not for political reasons, but because they hated the kind of narrow, strict conformist behaviour demanded by the Nazis. Their resistance took the form of refusing to join the Hitler Youth organisations, going on mixed camping trips and dressing very casually. These groups consisted mainly of working-class boys and existed in different places with different names, such as 'Roving Dudes' and 'Navajos'. Some, more middle-class, youths listened to 'forbidden' American jazz and 'swing' music in bars and nightclubs. There was no single organisation that they joined and no leaders, but the Nazis tended to refer to non-conformist youths as the **Edelweiss Pirates**.

During the Second World War the number of these non-conformist youths seems to have increased and concern grew after 1942 as their activities became more political — daubing anti-Nazi graffiti on walls, stealing weapons and even helping army deserters and escaped prisoners of war. In December 1942 over 700 were arrested in Düsseldorf and many were sent to labour camps. In Cologne in 1944, 12 Edelweiss Pirates were hanged publicly following the murder of the head of the Cologne Gestapo.

Only a relatively small number of young people were ever involved in such activities but they do provide evidence that the Nazis did not succeed in winning over the loyalty of all young Germans.

Questions

Use the information provided, your class notes and your textbook to answer the following questions.

1 What was the overall aim of the Nazis' policies towards young people?

2 Why were young people so important to the Nazis?

3 How did the Nazis attempt to control what young people thought and believed?

4 Describe **two** steps the Nazis took to control what went on in schools.

5 Describe **three** examples of beliefs children were expected to develop through the subjects they studied in school.

6 What special educational institutions were set up for young people who showed the potential to become future leaders?

7 How was the Hitler Youth movement organised?

1

2

3

4

5

6

7

Questions

8 Complete the table about Hitler Youth activities.

Example of HJ activity	What young people were meant to learn/develop from it

9 Why did the Nazis decide to make the Hitler Youth movement compulsory when they already controlled schools? Give at least **three** reasons.

9

Source questions

10 What does Source A tell us about the aims of education in Nazi Germany?
- Do not just describe what the picture shows. What can be *inferred/deduced* from it?

Source A

A picture from a Nazi school book for young children

10

THE WIENER LIBRARY

Questions

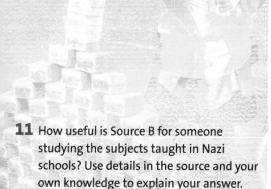

Source B

A pilot on take-off carries twelve bombs, each weighing ten kilos. The plane flies to Warsaw (capital of Poland and centre for Jews). It bombs the town. On take-off with all bombs on board and 1,500 kilos of fuel, the aircraft weighed about eight tons. When it returned from the crusade, there are still 230 kilos of fuel left. What is the weight of the aircraft when empty?

A problem from a Nazi school textbook. Quoted in *Nazi Power in Germany* by Greg and Jean Thie, 1989

Source C

It has been estimated that as many as 95% of German youth backed the Nazis, or at least Hitler, and that opposition for the most part remained vague and diffuse.

From *Nazi Germany* by A. Witt, 1994. Quoted in *Weimar and Nazi Germany* by J. Hite and C. Hinton, 2000

11 How useful is Source B for someone studying the subjects taught in Nazi schools? Use details in the source and your own knowledge to explain your answer.

- Explain how the source is useful for showing the hidden aims of Nazi education and support your answer with reference to details in the source.
- Use your knowledge to point out other aims not evident in this source.

12 What does Source C suggest about the success of the Nazis in winning over the loyalty of young people to Nazism?

- What overall impression is given of the extent of Nazi success?
- What details suggest limits to this success?

11

12

Questions

13 How far does Source D contradict (suggest the opposite of) Source C? Use details in the source and your own knowledge to explain your answer.
- What different impression is given by this source of the success of the Nazis in winning over young people?
- Use your knowledge and details of the source to discuss the *extent* to which the sources suggest different things.

MARY EVANS PICTURE LIBRARY

Source D
The public hanging of 12 Edelweiss Pirates at Cologne in 1944

13

Extended writing

On separate paper, write a short essay in answer to the following question.

14 How successful were the Nazis in turning young people into supporters of Nazism? Use Sources A–D above and your own knowledge to explain your answer.

14 A very good answer will draw on details from the sources and background knowledge to:
- present evidence and arguments that suggest they were successful
- present evidence and arguments that suggest they failed
- come to a clear conclusion supported by reasons about the *extent* of their success or failure

Germany under Hitler was a **totalitarian state** — the Nazis wanted total control over people's lives, even to the point of controlling what German citizens could read, listen to, or see in cinemas and art galleries.

Propaganda

Propaganda is the spreading of selected ideas and information to make people think and believe what you want them to. It was used by the Nazis to maintain support for Hitler's government.

A special government department for propaganda was set up in March 1933 under **Josef Goebbels**, who became minister for popular enlightenment and propaganda. His job was to control what the German people thought and believed and to build up and maintain their support for Hitler.

Goebbels believed the key to effective propaganda was to keep the message simple, and to keep repeating it. Some simple beliefs the Nazis wanted all Germans to accept were:

- Hitler knew what was best for the German people.
- They were part of a **master race** and other races were inferior.
- Jews and Communists were responsible for Germany's past problems.
- The German nation was more important than individual people.

The Nazis took various steps to ensure that such things were believed. First they eliminated alternative viewpoints:

- School textbooks were rewritten to fit in with Nazi ideas (see Topic 6) and in May 1933 books by Jews, Communists and anyone the Nazis disapproved of were burned. New books could only be published if approved by Goebbels's ministry.
- In 1933 there were over 4,000 daily newspapers in Germany owned by different people and organisations. Socialist and Communist newspapers were taken over immediately or destroyed. Others were taken over gradually by the Nazi publishing company **Eher Verlag**, which owned two thirds of the German press by 1939. All news was controlled and censored carefully by the DNB, the state-owned press agency.

Second, Goebbels believed that propaganda was more effective if heard rather than read:

- By 1934 all radio stations were put under the control of the Reich Radio Company.
- Cheap radios ('**people's receivers**') were mass-produced to ensure that more families had one and by 1939, 70% of German households did — a higher proportion than any other country in the world at that time.
- The radio did provide light entertainment, but its most important function was to broadcast Hitler's speeches. Loudspeakers were placed in town squares, offices, factories and cafés to ensure that even those without radios would hear the Führer's words.

The cult of the Führer

People were more likely to accept Nazi ideas without question if they could be persuaded to see Hitler as a godlike figure. This was the purpose behind the cult of the Führer, which was constructed carefully. Portraits of Hitler appeared in all schools, government offices and public places. On his birthday, 20 April, his picture appeared in all newspapers and shop windows. He was portrayed in photographs and newsreels as a man who worked tirelessly for his country. Many historians believe that Hitler was, in fact, a rather lazy and inefficient leader. However, this image building was extremely successful and Hitler remained very popular with the majority of Germans. His appearances at public meetings invariably received a hysterical reception.

Such meetings and **mass rallies** were also used by the Nazis to consolidate their hold over the German people. Rallies like the annual one at Nuremberg in the autumn brought hundreds of thousands of people together for spectacular displays consisting of mass movement, flags and German music, sometimes with torch-light processions at night — all of which provided a charged, emotional atmosphere for promoting Hitler's image.

These rallies were intended to demonstrate the efficiency, order and discipline the Nazi regime had brought to Germany. Their aim was also to reinforce the loyalty of those who attended and to ensure that when they returned home they would spread the Nazi message with even greater enthusiasm.

Sport was given strong emphasis, especially in schools:
- Young women who were fit and healthy would produce fit and healthy children.
- Young men would one day be soldiers and could learn teamwork as well as improve fitness through sport.
- Many fit and healthy young people would show that the Germans really were a 'master race'.

The **Berlin Olympic Games of 1936** were used for propaganda to show the world the progress that had been made in Germany amd all persecution of Jews was suspended during the Games. The Olympics were a huge propaganda success and visitors were impressed with the efficiency of German organisation. Germany won more medals than any other country — but the 'master race' theory was undermined by the achievements of the star of the games, the black American athlete **Jesse Owens**, who won four gold medals.

Culture

In keeping with their other policies, the Nazis wanted to ensure that all aspects of cultural life were brought into line with their way of thinking. The freedom of expression and tolerance of the Weimar Republic gave way to strict government control. The Nazis' policy was to use the arts to put over their political ideas.
- **Art**. Only the work of 'approved artists' could be shown. All art connected to antiwar themes or social change was banned. Themes acceptable to the Nazis were forests, landscapes or peasants working in the fields; and historical or mythical images featuring blond, blue-eyed Aryan heroes and heroines. These images were meant to encourage national pride and fit in with the master race ideology (e.g. that physical strength was more worthy of value than intellectual ideas). 'Modern art' was dismissed as 'degenerate' (likely to corrupt people) and was removed from galleries.
- **Architecture**. Hitler disliked the **Bauhaus** school of architecture with its experimental designs, which had flourished in Weimar Germany. He preferred large, square public buildings of stone

with columns and steps like those in Ancient Greece and Rome, before which people would feel small. These buildings would reflect the strength, power and importance of the state over the needs of individuals.

- **Music**. All jazz music and the 'jitterbug' dance (both of which originated with 'racially inferior' black Americans) were banned. The works of classical German composers like Bach, Beethoven and, especially, Richard Wagner, and traditional German folk music, were encouraged.
- **Cinema**. The cinema was very popular in Germany. Goebbels, a film fan himself, understood how effective the cinema was as a means of spreading propaganda messages to masses of people. He disliked films with an obvious political message like *The Eternal Jew*, an anti-Semitic documentary in which the Jews were likened to disease-spreading rats. He preferred more subtle propaganda, as in *Jud Süss*, a film about an eighteenth-century Jew who ends up being hanged for his crimes — another anti-Semitic film but one with a story and characters with whom the audience could relate.

In 1944 the film *Kolberg*, featuring heroic German resistance to Napoleon, was made to inspire fighting spirit in the latter stages of the Second World War. The project was thought to be so important that 100,000 soldiers were withdrawn from the front lines to help make it.

Most films produced after 1933 were provided for entertainment rather than propaganda, but the Reich Film Chamber checked the content of all of them before they could be shown. However, newsreels that preceded the main film nearly always emphasised a new achievement of Hitler's government.

How successful were Nazi propaganda and culture?

- The Nazis certainly achieved total control over the public communication of news and ideas, and Hitler's personal popularity increased in the 1930s.
- Those who were already committed to Nazism may have had their loyalty strengthened by constant exposure to propaganda, but it is difficult to assess whether or not the uncommitted were won over by it — especially in a country where freedom of speech and freedom of the press had been destroyed and where the threat of the secret police was always present.
- Some historians believe that where propaganda promoted traditional German values, e.g. the importance of the family, it was more successful than where it challenged those values, e.g. anti-Church policies.
- It is clear that the Nazis achieved total control over cultural activities, but it is difficult to assess their success in influencing people's beliefs. Many people involved in the arts left Germany because they were not free to produce the work they wanted. These included the artist **Paul Klee** and the playwright **Bertolt Brecht**.
- In 1937 an exhibition including work by Van Gogh and Picasso was staged by the Nazis to illustrate the weaknesses of 'degenerate art'. This received far more visitors than another exhibition put on at the same time to illustrate the 'true' German art that had Nazi approval.

Use the information provided, your class notes and textbook to answer the following questions.

1 What is meant by 'propaganda'?

2 Why did the Nazis use propaganda?

3 Give **three** examples of the sorts of things the Nazis wanted the German people to believe.

4 Why did the Nazis want to create a 'cult of the Führer'?

5 How was this cult created?

6 Why was sport so important to the Nazis?

1

2

3

4

5

6

Questions

7 How did the Nazis try to control what people thought? Answer this question by writing your own notes on each of the types of control in the table.

Type of control	Notes
A special government department	
Books	
Newspapers	
Radio	
Mass rallies	

Questions

8 In what ways were the Berlin Olympic Games a propaganda success for the Nazis?

9 Why was the success of Jesse Owens not welcomed by the Nazis?

10 How did Nazi policies towards the arts differ from those of the Weimar Republic?

11 Complete the table by explaining how these examples of art and culture were used to reinforce Nazi ideas.

8

9

10

11

Example	Nazi belief it was meant to reinforce
Paintings of historical scenes with typical Aryan heroes	
Large public buildings of stone with classical features	
The banning of American jazz music	
Films like *The Eternal Jew* and *Jud Süss*	

Questions

Source A

The Berlin Olympics 1936

After an impressive ceremony at which Herr Hitler, General Göring and other Nazi leaders were present, the Olympic Games were brought to a conclusion. The crowd cheered Hitler and there were repeated shouts of 'Heil!' Then followed the singing of the National Anthem.... The organisation of the Games has been magnificent.

A report from an English newspaper, the *Yorkshire Post*, 17 August 1936

Source B

Hitler saw the Olympics as an opportunity to display the physical superiority of Germans as the master race, their organisational ability and to enhance (improve) the country's international status. The new Germany was on show; anti-Semitic propaganda was reduced whilst visitors were present.

From *Weimar and Nazi Germany*, a textbook for students by J. Hite and C. Hinton, 2000

Source questions

12 What impression of the Olympic Games is given by Source A?
- Describe the overall feelings the writer had about the Games

13 What different impression of the 1936 Olympic Games is given in Source B? Refer to both Sources A and B in your answer.
- Here you must compare the sources, saying *how* they differ. Quote details from both.
- Explain how the overall impressions of the two sources differ.

12

13

Questions

14 Why do you think Sources A and B give different impressions of the Olympic Games? Explain your answer using Sources A and B and your own knowledge.
  - Here you must explain why the sources differ, so think about the different purposes of the two authors, intended audience and publication date.

Extended writing

On separate paper, write a short essay in answer to the following question.

15 How successful were Nazi policies towards popular culture and the arts after 1933?

14

15 You could include the following in your answer and any other information of your own:
  - The Ministry for Popular Enlightenment and Propaganda was set up under Goebbels in March 1933.
  - In 1937 an exhibition of 'degenerate art' received more visitors than an exhibition of art that had Nazi approval.
  - By 1939, 70% of all German homes had a radio.

The Nazis held strong **racial beliefs**:

- They believed that they were part of a separate northern European race called the **Aryan race** which was superior to all other races and so had to be kept pure.
- The ideal members of the Aryan race had certain physical features — they were tall, lean and strong with blond hair and blue eyes — but they were also intelligent, with a great capacity for hard work.
- Certain races, like the Jews and Slavs (peoples of central and eastern Europe), were inferior, and known as *Untermenschen* ('sub-humans').

The Nazis believed that to create a perfect community of healthy Aryans these racially inferior groups had to be dealt with. Other 'undesirable' minority groups also existed and they, too, could not be allowed to hold back the development of the 'master race'.

Treatment of minority groups

- In July 1933 a new law permitted the compulsory sterilisation of people with conditions the Nazis defined as hereditary illnesses such as 'simple-mindedness' and epilepsy. Chronic alcoholics could also be sterilised. About 350,000 people were sterilised over the following 12 years.
- Social groups that were not 'useful' and that were a 'burden' to the community were identified — such as tramps, beggars, the 'workshy' and homosexuals. These groups were called **asocials** and, over the years, most of them ended up in concentration camps where many died.

- The mentally ill were seen as 'unproductive' and costly to care for. In October 1939 **Operation T4**, a programme of **euthanasia** ('mercy killing'), began by killing registered mentally disabled children by starvation or lethal injection. The programme was extended to adults, and gas chambers were built in several asylums, but it was stopped in 1941 following public protests led by the Catholic Church. Techniques developed in the T4 programme were later used in the Holocaust.
- **Gypsies** were not regarded as a serious problem early in the Nazi regime because they numbered only about 25,000 in Germany. However, their different culture, lifestyle and racial mix made them 'outsiders' and in 1938 Himmler issued a decree for the 'Struggle against the Gypsy Plague', which introduced the compulsory registration of all gypsies. Together with other 'asocials', they were put into concentration camps after the Second World War began. It has been estimated that 500,000 gypsies from all over Europe died in the camps.

Why were the Jews persecuted?

The Nazis did not invent **anti-Semitism** (anti-Jewish feeling). It had been common in Germany and other countries for many centuries. Hitler may have developed his deep hatred of the Jews during his years in Vienna. Once in power he was in a position to make discrimination against Jewish people legal, a part of government policy. He and other Nazi leaders believed the Jews were:

- to blame for Germany's past problems, e.g. defeat in the First World War

- exploiting the German people because it was claimed (wrongly) that all Jews were wealthy businessmen, shop owners or bankers
- an inferior race that might damage the purity of the Aryan race

How were the Jews persecuted?

- **Through propaganda**. Jews were portrayed as enemies of the people and as being responsible for Germany's problems. These ideas were spread via Nazi newspapers such as *Der Stürmer*, posters, films (see page 59), anti-Semitic signs and speeches by Hitler and other Nazi leaders.
- **Through the education system**. Nazi control of education enabled them to put anti-Semitic material into the curriculum of every subject and into the classroom of every school in Germany. New subjects like 'race studies' were introduced, in which pupils learned to recognise Jewish racial characteristics.
- **Through government policies and laws**. In the early months of the Nazi regime anti-Semitic measures were random and unpleasant, but not yet violent. On 1 April 1933 a national boycott of Jewish shops and businesses was organised, but it had only a limited effect and was called off after 1 day. In the same month thousands of Jewish civil servants were sacked. Over the next 2 years signs began to appear in many public places such as swimming pools and parks saying 'Jews not wanted here'. Jewish teachers were sacked from state schools and Jewish musicians were banned from performing in public.

From 1935 onwards, however, discrimination against Jews became more formal:

- The **Nuremberg Laws** (September 1935) stated that Jews were no longer German citizens; marriage and sexual relationships between Jews and Aryans were forbidden.
- In April 1938 all Jewish-owned property had to be registered (in order to make it easier for the authorities to confiscate it later).
- In July 1938 Jewish doctors and dentists were barred from having Aryan patients.

Such measures were designed to remove Jews gradually from all areas of German life. However, November 1938 saw a serious escalation in the severity of Nazi treatment of Jews in the form of open violence.

Kristallnacht ('Night of Broken Glass')

In November 1938 a German embassy official called **Ernst von Rath** was murdered in Paris by a young Jewish boy, **Herschel Grynspan**. The Nazis claimed this was part of a wider Jewish conspiracy and on the night of 9 November the SA organised attacks on Jewish people and property throughout Germany. During this one night 91 Jews were murdered, over 200 synagogues burned and thousands of Jewish shops and businesses attacked and looted. An estimated 20,000 Jewish men were arrested and sent to concentration camps, and Jews were ordered to pay 1 billion marks to the government to cover the cost of the damage. After this, more laws were passed against them:

- 15 November 1938: all Jewish pupils were expelled from state schools.
- 3 December 1938: in Berlin, Jews were barred from all theatres, cinemas, sports grounds and other public places and were forbidden to walk or drive down certain streets.

Emigration of Jews from Germany

As the table opposite shows, thousands of Jews left Germany during the 1930s — in January 1939 the Reich Central Office for Jewish emigration was set up to encourage more to leave.

Year	Emigrants
1934	22,000
1935	21,000
1936	25,000
1937	24,000
1938	40,000
1939	78,000

Many more Jewish people might have left if foreign governments had been willing to take them. Those who stayed in Germany may have done so because they could not afford to emigrate. Others may have been reluctant to leave their homes and all their possessions, and just hoped things would get better. Despite the growing severity of discrimination against them, most German Jews were still living in their own homes until the mass transportation to death camps began in 1942.

The Second World War and the 'Final Solution'

The onset of the war in September 1939 marked another turning-point in Nazi treatment of the Jews. After the invasion of Poland in 1939 and Russia in 1941, millions more Jews fell into the hands of the Nazis. To deal with this growing 'Jewish problem' the Nazis adopted three new measures:

- In Poland, in October 1939, Jews were forced into walled **ghettos** in towns and cities, the largest being in Warsaw. Thousands died of starvation in these ghettos.
- In Russia, special squads of SS soldiers called ***Einsatzgruppen*** rounded up the Jews in a particular area, shot them and buried them in mass graves. Some were locked inside lorries and gas was pumped inside. This was the beginning of the systematic mass murder of Jews.
- From September 1941 all Jews were ordered to wear the Star of David.

The 'Final Solution' to the 'Jewish problem' — to murder all of them — was probably planned during 1941, but the details were agreed at a conference at **Wannsee** in Berlin in January 1942. **Death camps** were built in occupied Poland where Jews were killed in specially constructed gas chambers. The location of these camps is shown on the map on page 68.

Over the following 3 years an estimated 6 million Jews from all over Europe died in these camps — an episode in history that has become known as the **Holocaust** ('burning' or 'sacrifice') or **Shoah** ('destruction').

What made it possible for the Nazis to carry out the Holocaust?

- The Holocaust was made physically possible by the railway system which enabled the transportation of huge numbers of people directly to the death camps, packed into goods wagons.

Nazi concentration and extermination camps in Germany and German-occupied territories

Jews, and the building, maintenance and supplying of the death camps.

Resistance

- In April 1943 a few hundred Jewish fighters in **Warsaw** fought against a much larger and better-armed force of German soldiers who were attempting to round up the Jews in the city and send them to concentration camps. They held out for a month until the uprising was crushed.
- In October 1943 a revolt in the camp at **Sobibor** led to the escape of dozens of prisoners.
- In the camps and ghettos people resisted by continuing to practise their faith as best they could.
- Some Germans, too, resisted by sheltering Jews. One man, **Oskar Schindler**, saved the lives of hundreds through his 'list' of special workers.

- It was politically possible because of the vast areas of Europe that the Nazis occupied by 1942. Until the tide of war went against them there was no one to stop them.
- It was made humanly possible by the fact many thousands of Germans (and sometimes people of other nationalities) cooperated with it — not just soldiers and camp guards, but others involved with the railways, the identification and rounding up of

The end of Nazi Germany

By early 1945 Allied forces were closing in on Germany. On 27 January 1945 Russian soldiers reached the camp at **Auschwitz-Birkenau** and liberated surviving prisoners there. Hitler shot himself on 30 April 1945, with Russian soldiers only a short distance away from his bunker in Berlin.

Questions

Use the information provided, your class notes and your textbook to answer the following questions.

1 According to the Nazis, what was special about the Aryan race?

2 What were the ideal members of the Aryan race like?

3 Complete the timeline by matching the following jumbled events with the correct dates.

- Jews barred from many public places in Berlin
- Nuremberg Laws introduced
- Russian soldiers liberate Auschwitz concentration camp
- Jews ordered to wear Star of David
- Boycott of Jewish shops; Jewish civil servants sacked
- Uprising by Jews in Warsaw Ghetto
- *Kristallnacht* — attacks on Jewish property and synagogues
- Revolt by Jewish prisoners in Sobibor death camp
- Polish Jews forced to move into ghettos
- Wannsee Conference — details of death camps agreed
- Jewish doctors and dentists barred from having Aryan patients

1 ....

2 ....

....

3

Date	Event
April 1933	
September 1935	
July 1938	
November 1938	
December 1938	
October 1939	
September 1941	
January 1942	
April 1943	
October 1943	
January 1945	

4 Explain how the following events marked important turning-points in Nazi policies towards the Jews:

a *Kristallnacht*

b the German invasions of Poland and Russia

4a

_____

_____

_____

b

_____

_____

_____

5 Complete the table about the persecution of minority groups.

Minority group	Why they were persecuted	How they were persecuted
Asocials, e.g. tramps, beggars		
Mentally disabled		
Gypsies		
Jewish people		

Questions

6 Why didn't more Jews leave Germany before the Second World War began?

6

7 Define briefly each of the following terms as used in this topic:
a the Aryan race
b asocials
c euthanasia
d anti-Semitism
e *Einsatzgruppen*
f the Holocaust

7a

b

c

d

e

f

8 Name the main death camps set up after 1942.

8

9 Describe briefly **three** examples of resistance to the Nazi persecution of Jews during the Second World War.

9

Source A

1 Marriages between Jews and German citizens are forbidden.
2 Sexual relations outside of marriage between Jews and German citizens are forbidden.

The Law for the Protection of German Blood and Honour, introduced on 15 September 1935

Source B

The announcement of the death of the diplomat Von Rath by the cowardly hand of the Jewish murderer has aroused spontaneous demonstrations throughout the Reich. In Berlin, as in other parts of the Reich, drastic anti-Jewish demonstrations have taken place. In many places Jewish shop windows have been smashed...and synagogues set on fire.

From a German newspaper report of *Kristallnacht*, 10 November 1938

Source C

The rioting began in the early hours of the morning when formations of the Hitler Youth and SA streamed out of the taverns where they had been celebrating the anniversary of Hitler's march on Munich.... Synagogues were fired... gangs stumbled through the streets hurling bricks and stones through the windows of Jewish shops.... The average Germans looked on either apathetic or astonished. They passed scenes of destruction half-ashamed.

From an English newspaper report of *Kristallnacht*, 11 November 1938

Source questions

10 What does Source A tell you about Nazi policies towards the Jews?
  ■ Do not just describe what the source says. What can be *inferred/deduced* from it?

11 Study Sources B and C. How far do these accounts of *Kristallnacht* agree? Use details from Sources B and C and your own knowledge to explain your answer.
  ■ Note points that the sources agree on.
  ■ Note points where they seem to disagree.
  ■ Which seem more important — the points of agreement or disagreement? Use your knowledge of this event and come to a clear conclusion that answers the question.

10

11

Questions

12 Why was the cartoon in Source D published? Use the source and your own knowledge to explain your answer.

- Use details from the cartoon and your knowledge of the historical context to support your argument.

Extended writing

On separate paper, write a short essay in answer to the following question.

13 How far did Nazi policies towards Jewish people change from 1933 to 1945? Use Sources A–D and your own knowledge to explain your answer.

Source D

THE WIENER LIBRARY

A cartoon from a children's book, 1938

12

13 | **Guidelines**
A very good answer will:
- use details from named sources to illustrate changes up to 1939
- use additional knowledge to explain changes after 1939
- come to a clear, supported conclusion that considers the extent of the changes in policy

This enquiry in depth focuses on a period of 26 years — an extremely short time in historical terms but one that had a huge influence on the history of the twentieth century and that has helped shape our world today.

It is easy to get bogged down in detail when you study history and so the purpose of this final topic is to help you stand back and see the 'big picture' of this period of German history. This section is, therefore, divided into two parts:

- 1919–January 1933: the years of the Weimar Republic and Hitler's rise to power
- 1933–45: the years of the creation and establishment of the Nazi dictatorship

1919–January 1933

- The Weimar Republic was created in 1919. It was the most democratic government Germany had ever had.
- The Republic was disliked by many Germans from the beginning because of its association with defeat in the First World War and the Treaty of Versailles.
- There were several attempts in the early years to overthrow the Republic — by left-wing groups, e.g. the Spartacists, and right-wing groups, e.g. the Kapp Putsch and the Munich Putsch.
- The Republic also had to deal with severe economic problems, especially the inflation crisis of 1923.
- Despite these problems, the Weimar Republic survived and enjoyed a period of recovery and improved relations with other countries under the leadership of Stresemann from 1924 to 1929.

- This recovery was highly dependent on US loans, which ended with the Wall Street Crash.
- The Crash was followed by a period of rising unemployment, which had reached 6 million by 1932.
- This was accompanied by growing support in elections for extremist parties — most notably the Communist Party and Hitler's National Socialists.
- Growing political instability led to President Hindenburg becoming increasingly involved in the government of Germany (e.g. 'ruling by decree') and finally appointing Hitler as chancellor in the belief that other politicians could control him.

Historians disagree as to whether or not the Weimar Republic could have survived and Hitler's rise to power could have been prevented. Some argue that the Republic never really had the full support of the German people, especially the influential business and landowning classes. Therefore, once the Depression was under way it was increasingly likely that the Weimar Republic would have been replaced by some other form of government. Others believe that if Hitler had not been appointed by Hindenburg the Nazis would have gone into decline, especially as there were signs at the end of 1932 that support for them in elections was falling and the economic situation was improving.

1933–45

- January 1933–August 1934 saw the final destruction of the democratic Weimar Republic and the **creation of Hitler's dictatorship**. Key events in this process were: the Enabling

Law (1933), which gave Hitler the power to make laws without consulting the Reichstag; the Night of the Long Knives (30 June 1934), which saw the elimination of SA leaders and other potential rivals to Hitler's power; and the death of President Hindenburg (August 1934), which left Hitler as Führer — sole leader of Germany.

- Immediately after Hitler was made chancellor, in January 1933, the process of tightening Nazi **control** over the political system and the media began. The setting up of the Gestapo and SS created a police state, which was a major reason for the lack of opposition in the years up to 1939. However, **opposition groups** began to emerge during the war years.
- Nazi aims for the **economy** in the early years were to reduce unemployment and rebuild Germany's armaments and military forces. Many sections of German society benefited from the economic recovery that followed. After 1936 the main priority was to prepare for war — although it is almost certain that Hitler only expected a short war in eastern Europe. The fact that it became a long, drawn-out world war had devastating effects on the German economy and people, and led to the final collapse of the Nazi dictatorship.
- **Women** had a very clear role in Nazi Germany — to reverse the falling birth rate and produce as many children as possible. Many measures were introduced to encourage early marriage and raise the status of motherhood. At the same time a programme of compulsory sterilisation was introduced to ensure that 'unsuitable' women did not produce children.
- The Nazis had no interest in **religion** but failed in their efforts to reduce the importance of Christianity in Germany.

- Hitler was determined that Nazi beliefs would be passed on to each new generation. This, therefore, became the main function of the **education** system. To ensure this happened, the curriculum was reorganised with the introduction of new subjects like race studies, and textbooks were rewritten so they conformed to Nazi ideas. The indoctrination of young people into Nazism continued in the evenings and at weekends through the further development of the **Hitler Youth** movement, which also introduced elements of military training. The attempt to win over the younger generation was not entirely successful, as shown by the activities of **non-conformist** youths, especially after 1939.
- **Propaganda** was the main means by which the Nazis tried to ensure that the German people thought and believed as they wanted. **Goebbels** took the main responsibility for this. Newspapers, radio, films, mass rallies, art and even the Berlin Olympics were used for propaganda purposes.
- The Nazis aimed to create a nation of pure Aryans — a **superior race**. This led to the ill-treatment of groups thought likely to obstruct this mission — the mentally ill, asocials, gypsies and, most especially, Jews. Persecution came in many forms — from discrimination to violence and, ultimately, the 'Final Solution' from 1942 onwards.

The final collapse of the Nazi regime was brought about by defeat in war. Although there were attempts on Hitler's life, such as the July Bomb Plot of 1944, there was no sign of an uprising by the German people against the government, even in the final months of the Second World War.

Questions

Use the information provided, your class notes and your textbook to answer the following questions.

1 Complete the timeline by writing the following events in the correct order, adding the relevant month when more than one event occurred in the same year.

- Hitler attempted a putsch in Munich
- Germany joined the League of Nations
- Kapp attempted a putsch in Berlin
- The Nazis won 196 seats in an election
- The Wall Street Crash occurred
- Hitler was made chancellor of Germany
- Ebert was elected as the first president of the Weimar Republic
- The Dawes Plan arranged loans from the USA
- Hitler won 13 million votes in a presidential election against Hindenburg
- French troops occupied the Ruhr
- The Nazis won 230 seats in an election
- Stresemann became chancellor of Germany
- The Treaty of Versailles was signed
- The Nazis won 107 seats in an election
- Hindenburg was elected president of Germany
- Hitler became leader of the NSDAP
- The Nazis won 28 seats in an election

1

Year	Month (if relevant)	Event
1919		
1919		
1920		
1921		
1923		
1923		
1923		
1924		
1925		
1926		
1928		
1929		
1930		
1932		
1932		
1932		
1933		

Questions

2 All the labels shown in this table are in the correct column but not in the correct chronological order. Complete the table on pages 78–79 by writing each event in the correct place. You may need to look back through the workbook to find the dates.

Control/ opposition	Economy	Women and Church	Education/youth	Propaganda/culture	Persecution of Jews and others
Night of the Long Knives	Unemployment down to 0.5 million	Euthanasia criticised by Bishop of Münster	Edelweiss Pirates executed in Cologne	Exhibition of 'degenerate art'	*Kristallnacht*
White Rose movement in Munich	Albert Speer in charge of armaments	Martin Niemöller arrested	HJ membership made compulsory	Berlin Olympics	Wannsee Conference
Enabling Law	Four-Year Plan began	Women had to register for war work	Political activities by Edelweiss Pirates	70% of homes had 'people's receivers'	Auschwitz liberated/end of Second World War
July Bomb Plot	Bombing of Dresden	Marriage Law introduced	HJ membership reached 8 million	Propaganda film *Kohlberg* made	Boycott of Jewish businesses
Reichstag Fire	Hjalmar Schacht put in charge of economy	Sterilisation programme started	Ministry of Education created in Berlin	Goebbels put in charge of propaganda	German invasion of Poland/start of Second World War
Hindenburg died	Conscription introduced	Encyclical of Pius XI	HJ membership rose to 3,500,000	Radio stations put under Nazi control	Nuremberg Laws passed

2

Date	Control/opposition	Economy	Women and Church
1933			
1934			
1935			
1936			
1937			
1938			
1939			
1940			
1941			
1942			
1943			
1944			
1945			

Questions

Date	Education/youth	Propaganda/culture	Persecution of Jews and others
1933			
1934			
1935			
1936			
1937			
1938			
1939			
1940			
1941			
1942			
1943			
1944			
1945			

Questions

3 Who am I? Write the names of the individuals (or groups) from the following list to whom each quote refers in the spaces provided:
- Heinrich Himmler
- Franz von Papen
- Gustav Stresemann
- Gertrude Scholtz-Klink
- Friedrich Ebert
- Paul Hindenburg
- The Edelweiss Pirates
- Josef Goebbels
- Wolfgang Kapp
- Leni Riefenstahl
- Hermann Goering
- Jesse Owens
- Hjalmar Schacht
- Jehovah's Witnesses
- The Spartacists
- Hans and Sophie Scholl
- Claus von Stauffenberg
- Baldur von Schirach
- Martin Niemöller
- Ernst Röhm

3a 'I upset Hitler by winning four gold medals in the Berlin Olympics of 1936.' ....

b 'I was in charge of propaganda while Hitler was in power.' ....

c 'We led a student opposition group in 1942 called "White Rose".' ....

d 'I led the recovery in Germany from 1924 to 1928.' ....

e 'I was a priest who criticised the Nazis in 1937.' ....

f 'Members of our religious group refused to join the German Army. Many of us died.' ....

g 'I helped persuade Hindenburg to make Hitler chancellor in 1933.' ....

h 'I directed a propaganda film about the Nuremberg Rally of 1934.' ....

i 'I was in charge of the Hitler Youth.' ....

j 'We attempted a Communist rising in Germany in 1919.' ....

k 'I was leader of the SA until the "Night of the Long Knives".' ....

l 'I was in charge of Hitler's SS.' ....

m 'We refused to join the Hitler Youth and painted anti-Nazi slogans on walls.' ....

n 'I was head of all women's organisations after 1934.' ....

o 'I was president of Germany from 1925 to August 1934.' ....

p 'I was the army officer who led an attempt to kill Hitler in 1944.' ....

q 'I was in charge of rebuilding the German economy from 1934 to 1937.' ....

r 'I led a right-wing putsch against the Weimar Republic in 1920.' ....

s 'I was in charge of the Four-Year Plan from 1936.' ....